*To My Precious Grandchildren
Anand, Shaan & Leela*

Written by Arati Sinha
Illustrated by Mukul Naidu

Leela

Under a coconut grove, in a little red house, lived a little girl named Leela.

Leela was a happy girl. Every morning Leela said:
"Good morning, Mama."
"Good morning Leela," Said Mama.

"Good morning, Papa."
"Good morning Leela,"
Said Papa.

"Good morning, cuckoo bird Picku."
"Ckoo, Ckoo,
Good morning Leela,"
Said cuckoo bird Picku.

"Good morning, baby cow Puffy."
"Moo, Moo,
Good morning Leela,"
Said baby cow Puffy.

"Good morning, baby Duck Kutkut."
"Quack, Quack,
Good morning Leela,"
Said baby duck Kutkut.

"Good morning, baby elephant Ramba."
"Roar, Roar,
Good morning Leela,"
Said baby elephant Ramba.

"Good morning, baby frog Ricky."
"Ribbit, Ribbit
Good morning Leela,"
Said baby frog Ricky.

"Good morning, baby goat Ziffy."
"Baa, Baa,
Good morning Leela,"
Said baby goat Ziffy.

"Good morning, baby horse Happy."
"Neigh, Neigh,
Good morning Leela,"
Said baby Horse Happy.

"Good morning, baby kitten Shino."
"Meow, Meow,
Good morning Leela,"
Said baby kitten Shino.

"Good morning, baby monkey Koko."
"Hoo, Hoo,
Good morning Leela,"
Said baby monkey Koko.

"Good morning, little puppy Timtim."
"Woof, Woof,
Good morning Leela,"
Said little puppy Timtim.

"Good morning, baby Parrot Sumu."
"Tweet, Tweet,
Good morning Leela,"
Said baby parrot Sumu.

"Good morning, baby rabbit Tutu."
"Purr, Purr,
good morning Leela,"
Said baby rabbit Tutu.

Every evening Leela played with her friends:

Picku the Cuckoo bird,
Puffy the baby cow,
Kutkut the baby duck,
Ramba the baby elephant,
Ricky the baby frog,
Ziffy the baby goat,
Happy the baby horse,
Shino the baby Kitten,
Koko the baby monkey,
Timtim the little puppy,
Sumu the baby Parrot and,
Tutu the baby Rabbit.

They all made a big circle and danced with a big smile.

Draw Leela with Your Favorite Animals!

www.ingramcontent.com/pod-product-compliance
Lightning Source LLC
LaVergne TN
LVHW081509060526
838201LV00056BA/3023